The Sisters

The Sisters

New and Selected Poems

Josephine Jacobsen

 THE BENCH PRESS

These poems appeared in the following periodicals: *Commonweal:* "Distance" and "The Steps"; *Cross-Currents:* "The Strangers"; *New Letters:* "Characters in Motion" and "Now"; *The New Yorker:* "The Lovers," "Short Views in Africa," and "Sea Fog"; *Poetry:* "A Dream of Games"; *Southern Poetry Review:* "Reading Aloud at Dusk"; *Tri-Quarterly:* "Moon" and "Tiger"; *Yankee:* Interrogation." "Briefing for Finisterre"; Phi Beta Kappa poem, William and Mary College, 1978. The poems that appeared in the following publications are reprinted with the permission of the publisher: *The Animal Inside* (Ohio University Press, 1966); *The Chinese Insomniacs* (The University of Pennsylvania Press, 1981). The poems that appeared in *The Shade-Seller* (Doubleday, 1974) are registered in the name of Josephine Jacobsen.

Library of Congress Cataloging in Publication Data

Jacobsen, Josephine.
   The Sisters : new and selected poems.

   I. Title.
PS 3519.A424S484 1987 811'.52 86–20664
ISBN 0–930769–03–1
ISBN 0–930769–04–X (PBK.)

For Eric, yet again

Contents

From *The Animal Inside*

The Sisters

The Sisters

Everyone notices they are inseparable.
Though this isn't quite so, it might well be.
Talk about depending on each other . . .
One can't say they are totally
congenial— irritation isn't unknown.

Yet it is, truly, touching, how they go on
year after year, not just pairing lives but
taking even holidays and vacations together,
sharing what happens to come along.
Here they are in the Caribbean.

Choose a day— the eighteenth of March for example:
they awake at almost but not quite
the same instant, disoriented:
where is the east?   where anything else?
But they aren't going to dog each other all day.

B, anyone would have to admit,
is the better adjusted— easily pleased.
What marvelous lobster! she cries.
Smell the air!   (The island is full of spices
and the air is soft as well as fragrant.)

A's energy always seems to be erratic:
first she's on and on about something,
then she wants a nap.   She's a great sleeper
and has been known to cast away
hour after precious hour asleep without shame.

And she gets fixations— dashing off
to some spot they've already seen,
and talking about it when she gets back.
Take the little group of graves by the Old Men's Home
the station-wagon passes on its way to the beach.

Both of them noticed it— how could they help?
It's a little patch, unfenced, with four or five
graves.   One apparently new and covered
with brightness.   They even both waved
to the four old men on the porch who waved back.

But later, it turns out, *A* went back by herself,
sharp-eyed as ever, to examine the yellow
and violet cellophane, the rubber pond-lilies
floating on dust;   the whole glittering heap
of rainbow mound;   even asked questions.

That happened this morning;   with the result
that when *B* swam in the sea— that sea
like a sapphire flawed with gold and green—
A went to sleep.   The time she wastes
like that, slack as a weed in a wave!

This means that tonight she'll keep *B* awake
probably for hours, prowling about.
But they fight less than most sisters
and when the question of separation once arose
you should have seen them recoil— both, both.

At scrabble this afternoon they played partners:
tiles smooth to the fingertips, words appear-
ing, solid as objects— *salmon, cat*;   or abstract,
as *who, why, go*. They did very well.
Then *A* wouldn't participate in the talk at dinner.

On the whole, this was a good day;   hard rain
rattled the roof, then the real rainbow threw up its arch,
and amicably they watched the blood-orange dip
into water;   then stars, larger and brighter than elsewhere.
Before bed, *A* looked at herself in the mirror, using *B*'s eyes.

The Swimmers

They do not swim alone:
tri-colored, the water is deep,
the invisible tide strong.   They stay
near the pier.   Sharks never come in.

Little Miss Piper, Mr. Pruett
with the stomach, hairy Mr. Gray,
and the children who must constant-
ly be called back.

In the Caribbean they move in tides
come from over the bones of boys,
of girls gone down, of skeletal
galleons;   the necropolis of the fish.

Out of its glitter and sparkle
they rise to the day, to the palms'
sparkle and glitter;   brilliant with drops,
they step onto the ground.

So, out of the deeps of sleep
where they cannot keep company—
chosen, at least—
from the fathoms of memory, one

by one, at morning, they rise
into themselves, into their limbs, the new
sight of the old sun on their sea.
As though they would, always, wake.

The Chosen

(Grenada)

The sick are coming the sick are coming!
Today is the healing of the sick.   It is
today's Good News;   there has been preparation.
In this church all the chairs have arms.

Brought by the strong, the sick will come in last.
Out there the beach is a perfect blaze; no normal
rainbow ever carried more colors than this Caribbean,
and the almond blossoms are blowing; they fall

on the sand, in the wind that wildly flattens
the candle-flames in their glass.   Hibiscus
is seen through the brick-lace walls, red
as the little girls' barrettes: you could go on

with the sky, and their blue ribbons; and certainly
the clouds have the same white-white as their tall socks.
The faces, color of cocoa, obsidian, sand,
of bark, of nutmeg, are turned toward the door:

the choir, quiet, seethes with intention.   Now!
Between two of the strong, the sick ones creep:
lame, mostly; enormously tough and fragile,
like dark, bent-over birds.   Some

spectacular ravages; but sadly, largely
it turns out, the undramatic wounds of age.
They are lowered into chairs with dignity.
A tiny old woman chatters, chatters,

part prayers, part anecdotes to an
invisible friend. *Kumbaya*! the choir bays,
drowning the mocking-bird exulting
in health in the eucalyptus.

They lowered the leper through the roof, says the gospel,
because of the crowd.   The lifted faces, intent,
savor this: part of the roof, right off—
and there is the leper!   The next thing

you know, he has taken up his bed and gone
home.   The faces are raised to that story.
They believe it could happen; did happen; but
will not, right now.   The black tall priest

his sash embroidered with nutmeg bursting
through its mace, says he will bring them oil,
the oil of healing; and he does, bending, huge
and gentle. *Amen*!   *Amen*!   *It shall be so*!

shouts the choir: *hallowed be Thy name*!
Amen! *Amen*! *It shall be so*!   It has a beat
like Carnival; is a kind of road-march:
the foreheads, the palms, are raised to the oil,

a huge wave lifts the entire place:
fronds that swing in the sun, the enormous
healthy day, the loud bird
in its tree.   They are healed, healed:

they understand something I cannot:
that they wait: are loved: are in the palm
of the good power that chose their affliction.
Pray for us, the priest tells them, *You are closer to God*.

The bright chatterer pushes herself up
and begins to dance: a tiny road-march jump-up;
a Sister swirls, all veil and beads, to take her
claws, and down the aisle away they go like partners.

Now the Host rises, white and round
in the beautiful long black fingers
and even the choir is stricken
silent.   Given: a new Body.

Power! *Kingdom*!   shouts the choir
suddenly, *Glory*!   The guitar goes
fast and deeper.   *It shall be so!*
It shall be so!
                    The healthy leave first,

not to hurry the honored, in their slow
return to familiar sheets. If the terms of the contract
remain mysterious, it is signed.   The chosen
wait in their chairs for those not chosen.

Briefing for Finisterre

for Anne Healey

Do not be concerned with the black hole—
its density can only confirm truth—
or the ashy world of a particular planet,
or the scanner from a neighboring galaxy.

When you are taken— and you will be—
beyond Finisterre, say to yourself, "grass."
Remember it; love is a secret, only you
know what is inside it.   Remember that.

To be sure of what you will not give up
is the point.   Preparation is simple:
identify what you will not renounce.
Hold a secret.   Hold a blade of grass.

Phi Beta Kappa Poem, December 1978

The Edge

The edge?   The edge is:
lie by the breath you cannot
do without; while
the breather sleeps.

Precious, subtle, that air
comes, goes, comes.
The heart propels it.   It has
its thousands of hours, but

it will not last as long
as the sun, the moon's subservient
tides. It will stop, go back
to the great air's surround.

But now, subtle, precious,
regular as tide and sun
it moves in the warm body, lifts
the chest, says yes.

Listen to it, through the night.
If you wish to know the extent
to which you are vulnerable
only listen.

This is called the breath
of life.   But it continues
saving your life
through the dark,

since this engine that drives your joy
is unrenounceable.
Listen, listen.   Say, Love, love,
breathe so, breathe so.

The Suicides

There is much confusion about
the suicides: those who reject
us. It is those who take dark as an end

in itself who have that claim.   They put
the finger of darkness on all motion
towards or away, and on the changes

of blood or sun.   They have conquered
nature, where every insect, tiger, crab
fights death, this being the sole passion

shared absolutely.   Which beast
rejects life?   The hound, grieving
to death is only craving fresh

life for his master.   And we call
suicides those for whom the tunnel
of possibility has narrowed, closes

before them.   A gracious couple
enamored of life came to that tunnel's
end, and like Etruscan figures

lay side by side.   They wanted
nothing so much as life.   No;
the suicides belong to each other,

fraternal in solitude —
A rage of hunger for the void,
a shared lust for zero.

Being exclusively human, this is
like all humans, mysterious.
Without inducement the beasts live

to live.   Often "he/she had everything
to live for," we say.   This is the thing
itself; exclusively human.   Authentic.

Reading Aloud at Dusk

The small blind cripple's face was ready:
raised to receive the host of Mrs. Eddy.

Before the narrow house was tender dusk.
The dahlia-colored cat named Cheops licked his chops,

came into the room to the wheelchair and its dapper
sitter magnificent and fragile as a grasshopper.

A flower, alive, with an African name, grew noiseless
in a pot near my hand that held the printed voice.

I read how matter, how sin, is nothing, is not,
and Cheops unbuttoned his eyes behind my back;

the orange tom's squint face lit that dusk like a moon;
but the blind clear eyes stared straight through the room;

the blind clear eyes went forth to battle matter,
to liquidate the mantel   the pain   the table   the terror.

Never made flesh, the pure word rang like steel,
the corrupt clock ticked its tick and darkness fell.

A single roller-skate scoured the street and hushed;
the dark full violet rumpled its flowery flesh.

Pinned down in blackness, bright as a butterfly's flicker
she plunged her gleam like a knife in the void of matter;

washed with Mary Baker's smile the crucifix
to cleanse the shadow from the empty sticks.

The Motion

for Nancy Sullivan

The geranium in my studio window
with its blaze of faceted globe
has put up another bloom,
not open.   Red loose buds on top;
the tight green buds below point down.

I know trick film can show me what
happened.   But that is fake.   The real motion
can't be seen.   If I had come at three
in the morning, at six, would I
have caught it moving?   No.   No.

It's like that game of Steps.   When you open
your eyes, everything stops.   But I want,
very much, to see it happen;
it's actual.   And it's a hint of what
goes on the whole time.   Without a sound.

The withering, too.   When does that begin?
What is the first motion of the turn? the with-
drawal?   It's like that June 22nd
green-blue day that turns over
without stir or whisper, to face winter.

If I could see it happen, I could
know when all tides tip; how luck
shifts; and when loss is ready.   When
you are saying goodbye to someone you think
you'll see next week.   And don't. Ever.

Tiger

for Bessie

Diamonds or broken saucepans interchangeable,
Susie's sprung rocker, or her heart's blood,
are safe by his hatred, Tiger understands.

Tiger is Susie's dog.   Tiger and Susie know
the street is wicked in old wicked ways;
the street is dangerous and covers the city.

Alley and bitch-mother are gone so long
Tiger has one live being in his city;   his paws
never touch the wicked pavement

he watches.   The dirt yard has a gray high
wood fence— over it fell a piece of meat rank
with poison.   Susie found it first.   Now she goes

into that yard with Tiger when he goes.
In his three years he hasn't seen a cat or dog
or human— wicked lives— but through the window.

The bell wheezes sometimes.   Tiger flies
flies through the air, slams against the door
with 25 dog-fight noises in his teeth:

is dragged away, is shut upstairs, paces
paces paces in rage.   But then blessed the bolt
shoots home, the chain jingles.   Tiger shoots

down the stairs to his window, his glass; his glass
where he can watch the wicked at their ways,
who all are bad, will never be better, cannot come

in;   because Tiger the Judge, unmated, single
in intent, will tear them to shreds to scatter
at Susie's cracked shoe.   He has seen a dog

trotting like a Doppelgänger-enemy past and past;
or a dog in a room in the window, when at dark
the bulb is lit.   His joys are Susie's step on the three steps

he has never gone down. There's a time his tongue
drips; that's summer.   Then there is the time
the gas-jets on the stove stay bright all night.   Tonight

snow vibrates along the street and changes it:
but not the wicked, waiting behind their walls
to rob, to murder, or to visit.   The snow is like a pulse

a hypnotizing pulse.   And Tiger lets himself
fall on his side by Susie's salvaged ankle
and lets the outside fill with snow and his eyes close.

A Dream of Games

I   A Game of Scrabble

His fingers hesitate over
his row— it is stammering
with i   i   i.   Here nothing can stand
alone, let alone i.
Insipid, he finally puts
and judgment
leaps on the board with a sweep.

The tall child makes *gory*, doubled.
The smooth tiles spell
relationships, accidents.
...*eath*, ...eath.   Fingering
a *d*, one pauses here.   A *d*
would do; *br* would be better.

Beyond the balcony the sea
flees in long quivers.   Now here is the *q*,
Friday before Crusoe— he has used his *u*
in *ruins*.
Below, slick and lovely, the frangipani
boughs black as snakes and bare, spring
into pink at the top.   Has anyone ever made
frangipani?

She has ...*ight*; the sea suggests
an *l*— the sailboats shed it, the mango shines it back,
br the mango says.   She has only an *n*
and the whole island disappears: where is the moon?
Not one thin star? *Delight*'s chance is lost.

Instead, *gone* appears; then *vein*,
now *vasty*.   Everything stops
for argument.   *Vasty?*   Halls, halls
of death, says the woman, wringing her rings.
The sun drops a little, but *vasty*
is removed, and there is *video.*   Two tiles
are left, *e*, *r*, and go on *lied.*   The man says
that is foreign, the woman says
songs are here.   There is no dictionary.
Lieder stays.

The woman has won.   The child is sad.   The man
looks at the words, connected, without context.
On the rail
the tiny dragon, alligator, lizard
over his eyes' black specks, smiles
and *lieder, death, vein, night*
just as the sun makes its move
to leave, shatter and meld and clatter
into the box.

II   A Bridge of Knaves

Knave says the book: *slippery,*
a shrewd fellow. Here, all dignity
stuffily clad, in profile or not quite,
hunts with the pack;

falls with no sound face-
down on felt.   Lifted,
takes on his rank, jaunty, reticent;
looks past the players.

Christened a club, so is he dark,
time-out-of-mind, if dates matter.   Club?
He prefers to claim deep chairs, deep rugs,
hot andirons, snow beyond glass; exclusions;

but his half-turn still says, too,
old caves, old hunts, new hunts; egg-shell
heads, egg-shell bones.   Say what he will
he stays the ancient heir.

The Diamond Knave that points
his almost-smile, says, glitter
on velvet or flesh like velvet; cut
or be cut.   True, rain and sun

fling *trompe-l'oeil* imitations,
flash-and-go, and bastard cousins,
terrapin, rattler, carry
that family insignia.

The lips of the Knave of Hearts tilt
up. What he has is different.
He cannot set a necklace, break
a head, play the grave-digger;

variety is his claim.   He says
his 3-inch sac will give you
an empire, a suicide; says it
has the ultimate connections, last and first.

Three Knaves know how absurd
is the fourth's eminence:
Spade must be the dealer's irony;
yokel, upraised.

The root's, the earthworm's visitor,
the flower's clownish uncle.
But in cardboard, one-eyed and natty,
In the end, he says, depend on me.

III   A Dream of Games

The game is dreamed for the rules:
when dusk takes the green diamond
set in dust, even the players' ghosts
are gone: the three-bat swing; the ghost

that hitched its belt, its cap; dipped
for the resin, hid its paw; leaned
like a pointer toward the tools-
of-ignorance crouch.   In dark the rules wait it out.

The game we dream writes lines
where *love* means *nothing*, and *service*
is neither waiter, priest nor stallion,
and *let* is a net's whisper.

The game is dreamed for the rules.
Monte Alban's old rule dreamed
that ball-court from which the loser died.
Chaos, soft idiot, is close

as breath. But the games appear,
celestial in order; contracts we make
with light: the winner humbled,
the loser connected with his law.

Interrogation

All day
and sometimes in the hollow evening
in their tunnels the machines
have questioned me:
heart, belly, skull.
"Don't breathe . . ." they said.
Click.   "Breathe . . ."
They had it their way.

Flat on the silver
surface or up
against the shiny plate: "Don't
breathe . . ."   Count.   Click.
"Breathe." Not an inch's
shelter.

Now they know
nothing, nothing.
I gave my name, rank,
social security number.
They have all the sights.
I, the secrets.
Breathing, or not,
I have told them nothing.   Nothing.

Distance

Distance is our quack doctor.
Human animal, I marvel
at ants, busily skirting their dead,
and pigeons, chattily convening by the
body of a pigeon.   Freedom
from anxiety! cries something envious.

I found a child's skin, breathing,
wrapped around bones, a look
straight from the pit, lying on my doorstep.
And while it still breathed, merrily went
straight into the bright here.

It was not on my doorstep.   Space
held it away; over a sea, perhaps.
Or, for argument, say another city.
In time, we were exact; together.
It shared my instant. It was distant.
Distance was all I needed from the ant.

Saints can't grasp distance.
It eludes their senses
as though all theres were here.
I survive shame; and feel distance
gently gently as a priceless pain-killer
locate and disconnect reality.

You Can Take It With You

for Evelyn Prettyman

2 little girls who live next door
to this house are on their trampoline.
The window is closed, so they are soundless.

The sun slants   it is going away:
but now it hits full on the trampoline
and the small figure at each end.

Alternately they fly up to the sun,
fly, and rebound, fly, are shot
up, fly, are shot up up.

One comes down in the lotus
position.   The other, outdone,
somersaults in air.   Their hair

flies too.   Nothing, nothing, noth-
ing can keep them down.   The air
sucks them up by the hair of their heads.

I know all about what is
happening in this city at just
this moment; every last

grain of dark, I conceive.
But what I see now is:
the 2 little girls flung up

flung up, the sun snatch-
ing them, their mouths rounded
in gasps.   They are there, they fly up.

Presences

I   The Creatures

Here they are common as pebbles.   Tree-
frog; cat; lizard.   I have been near them
today.   This morning the cat, which is yellow,
trotted along the path, through the pineapple palms.

When the sun was at an angle, the lizard
espaliered against the wall's stucco, stayed
like that for minutes on end — his head
a little raised, his tail fading into nothing;

and later, by a small flashlight, I found
in its axil the tree-frog, big as a thumb,
green as green glass, pulsing with sound
so shrill it slit night's membrane like a shard.

I could have touched him.   It was the same date
in history for all of us, the same acre,
the same air of spice and salt: here we were.
I do not comprehend outer space

but it is smaller, I know, than this distance
between us, this mystery we carry.
(I have seen a lioness trot like a cat,
light, light, with the tail's tip up,

I have seen the lizard's eighth cousin
rise on its alligator joints, onto tippytoes
and run fast as a dog.)   But those were
in places strange to me.   Here we cohabit.

The cat trots, the lizard clings to the wall,
the frog slits the silence.   Close,
close, distance makes me dizzy
with its sumptuous refusals.

There is an awful grace in such mystery.
Galaxies are simpler.   To have such disguises
as we circle each other: on a path,
on pink stucco; in the crotch of green.

II   The Clouds

What must be said of clouds is: they are silent.
Their silence is flawless. They move
with irregular edges over the vast backdrop

steadily; or, at a moment, swiftly.   A sound
would destroy that thick fleece, the puffed
and sailing curves going fast and silent.

I have seen them from above, but felt
no closer; they never promised support.
Those turreted fields are not for you.

When they tear almost imperceptibly
apart, the quiet is immense and the fila-
ments disperse and atomize.

Stained by the moon, a copper
fringe drags off the whole affair
and the moon glares round and bright

but the clouds go on away; pile white
over star over star.   Release star after star.
I don't know any other choices so quiet.

When I lie flat on the ground I can feel
the stillness pass over my face.   It softens
the gravestones and darkens flower faces.

Death is equally silent but does not move.
I think a good thing to see before the quiet that is
motionless, would be the bright soundless motion.

This silence fills the ear like another music.
It appeases.   How much time in which to be
grateful is roughly sufficient?

III   Now

The light in the garden has changed since death
arrived.   Motionless; patient.   Everything has brightened.
He had passed through, of course, leaving a bird
stiff under the nasturtiums; in a borrowed voice

called from a distant phone; that sort of thing.
But now like the stone-worn pedestal of the sundial
he is there.   And what an effect on light:
the garden has taken on a gleam, a brilliance,

a flash as though the whole scene had undergone
its vernissage; the leaves glitter, separate; the flowers'
blood pulses in the petal, where lavish, grass burns
its green;   the shadows are laid on with exactitude.

It is impossible to recall all the muted colors.
A blind man struck by sight could not be more astounded
than eyes that take in this meticulous riot.
It is now.   And you have seen its particulars.

The Rich Old Woman

The threadbare young
with their tiny roots,

the young in their thin
small memories,

bless them, and pity;
You tell them, Turn Rich.

You, after deserts, jungles,
after the knife

in the midnight brain,
after the water-lily

on the golden water of noon;
after the treecrests, moving,

before the storm, you may
pity the meager memory,

the tremulous root;
those uninstructed by loss,

by the joy whose root
runs down to China

sending up thick blooms.
From your treasure

too heavy to count, yet counted,
counted; all that plunder

(inestimable, falling out
of the closet of sleep, of the dark,

the heart's pulse
adding it over and over,) trans-

parent before death's light:
faces welcome as water

to thirst, friends, defended
from oblivion; and havoc, havoc

survived like a twister —
power, flowing back

up the nerve, the vein;
what you have salvaged, stolen,

won on the toss, brought with you
from the sand, the salt wave,

the garden. All, all.
Pity the meager

young. They start out,
with their tiny horde,

their fistful of minutes. See them!
May the young grow rich.

From *Let Each Man Remember*

Winter Castle

I   This then shall be our April . . .

This then shall be our April—this black heap
Lifting its stones from these forgotten snows;
The winds of these white slopes shall weave our sleep
For summer breezes, and the owl that goes
Silent and swift from turret to black bole
Shall serve as nightingale.   And in the storm
When torches die and tempest shakes the soul
And branches crack and only love is warm,
This rage shall be our sweets of spring.   No birds
Shall sing at these cold casements, and the day
Will bring no sun to thaw such ice—but words
There shall be spoken here and in such way
Not all July as these shall burn so bright
Within this sorrowful and savage night.

II   Let be; enough . . .

Let be; enough; I am not yours tonight
To touch and take.   Though we lie neighbored here
A bitter wind has put the crows to flight
Seeking rare shelter and the stars cut clear
Upon the frosted earth.   I have escaped
In some uncommon way through the thick walls,
And I am many-minded, diverse-shaped:
I am the horses, hay-warmed in the stalls,
The snow-sagged spruces, and the starving hare
Coursing the slopes of snow.   It is not well
That you should hold my body with this care
And tell me things, as I were here to tell,

While I am distant, hunting in the chill
With wolves that run upon the hungry hill.

III   Knowing your body . . .

Knowing your body and the lines of it,
Knowing a portion of your heart, at worst,
There is a country in your mind unlit
By any torch of mine.   I have a thirst
Tonight to spy its wells, hunger to touch
My fingers to its fruit, desire to trace
Its dark horizons and to climb and clutch
Its dizzy goat-paths where the sharp winds race
And flying clouds are close; and if my lust
For finding things bring me a bitter view,
Why, I am one whom danger never thrust
Away from her so sharply as she drew;
Our hands together, on the cruel ground
I shall stand steadfastly, and make no sound.

Laurentides

I Virgin In Glass

The little Virgin, fitted out in white
Behind the glass
Set in the center of the cross's height,
Inhabits quietly her novel plight,
Far from the Mass.

Above her head the symbols of the Line —
Carved arrow,
Pincers and hammer — lie within the sign
Of a thorn circle, cut in blunt design,
Wooden and narrow.

Below her sheltered perch the jagged rocks
Girdle the cross;
Serenely pink-cheeked in her little box
She gazes wisely on the winter fox,
The summer moss.

She was installed with wreaths and holiday
In bright July,
Blessed by the priest, pleasured by noise and play;
Priest, games and summer come and go away.
Her scrutiny

Stays to encounter the uplifted gaze
Of kneeling men,
Of children such a doll can still amaze,

Of women come to bargain or to praise.
In blizzards, when

A moose, encouraged by the private snow
Treads somberly
Across her vision, she will meet his slow
and doubtful look, before he turns to go
Not wholly free.

II   By the Rock

Search in the quiet of this motionless spot
Past the submerged brown stone, the pallid knot
Of streaked thin lake-grass; seek beyond the small
And desolate leaf sequestered since its fall
In shallow water.   Furry mosses lock
The rotting stick in growth.   Here is the rock,
Bronzed, ridged and tinted.   This shall be to you
Refuge in thought — rock clung to by the blue
And red-rust lichen, glided over by
The flickering fish's circular pop eye,
Spotted with fleeing shadow from the wing
Of dragonfly.   The ripples shivering
Beneath the wind do not perturb its face,
Its silent aqueous life.   Remark this place.

III   This House

This house is a room — divided, but still a room,
Shining by light.   The floor hard-stung by the broom,
The china swan outswelling with shaggy bloom,

And especially the walls, give back a rich response
To the pulse of the sheltered flame that beats in its sconce —
The walls of silk-smooth birch that were growing once.

There is almost no sound.   The chipmunks are in the roof
And they cling and peer down, but their family life is aloof
As the moose that leaves print in the mold of his chiseling hoof.

Outside is the night.   Outside the forests begin,
With claw and fur, and the lakes, with webbed foot and fin;
The walls, the swan and the breathing lamp are within.

Now the rubbish is torn away, and the clogging vines
From the single plant are wrenched, and the warm light shines
On the pattern of life, lifting spare and unalterable lines.

Non Sum Dignus

This Sabbath, as all others, finds
The building hushed for love of God
Save where the thin man, counting, winds
    His watch, and children creak and nod

In crowded pews.   The money chinks
Discreetly in the moving plate;
Through the stained glass the sunlight winks
On Adam at the Garden-gate.

Hands reach for gloves and rosaries—
"The Mass is ended" comes so soon—
Beyond the window butterflies
Sprinkle with white the burning noon.

The ancient usual retreat
Takes down the steps the scattering horde;
Adam again has met defeat,
Has missed connections with the Lord.

But where the altar-candles die
Waits God, and in a corner prays
The last of heroes who will try
The Gate again in seven days.

Mississippi Anatomy

This land is red, its body is colored of blood,
It is lonely and red,
Only pines spring up.   From this barren and scarlet mud
Indifference is bred.

These stretches will form no alliance with starlight or noon;
With a sullen glow
This repulses the sun, it refuses the moon
And is ignorant of snow.

It proffers no proof of its nurture, no cornfield, no spire,
Not a dog, not a cart;
Silent, it draws with confused and reluctant desire
The inscrutable heart.

From *The Human Climate*

Death and the Turtle

The turtles in the big green bowl are reduced by one;
A turtle climbed out, got lost, is disappeared.
A meticulous search has not found her, she is woefully gone.
Off she crept— the small tail protruding, the small head upreared.

Three days hope was held; but it has vanished.   Securely
She may have tucked herself in her shell; unbidden
Came someone who had watched her foolhardy departure.   Surely
Death found the turtle, wherever she may have hidden.

Now in her small lost body, under her painted shell
He is entered the house, and it is touched with a curious illness;
With no matter what laughter and noise, what pretense all is well,
We move, little and strange, at the heart of a present stillness.

For Any Member of the Security Police

1

Let us ask you a few questions, without rancor,
In simple curiosity, putting aside
Our reactions or the rising of our gorge,
As a child asks, How does it work? As premise:

Some limitations you admit: sound-proofing
Is never perfect, hints rise from any cellar;
There are a —very— few for whom reshaping
Must be abandoned for that catch-all, death.

The capitulation-point (call it X_2)
In very strong young men, well-fed and finicky,
Is sometimes unbelievably delayed.
Most are much easier: women they love,

The children from their bodies' seed, are garden-paths
To the objective.   And humiliation
After the first betrayal, serves as breach
So that all others follow fairly freely.

We haven't yet discussed the top success,
The mind's invasion; that fierce citadel
Proverbially adamant to rack and fire,
To conjuration — even sometimes to love,

Now, by a postern-door, all solved so simply.
Nothing more formidable than a needle,
A pellet; the kindly country-doctor's tools.
Now, with this data in mind, if you could tell us . . .

2

Is there routine in this, like unlocking the desk
And running through the Baskets, In and Out,
Uncovering the typewriter: Memo to Miss Prout;
How was our average on yesterday's task?

The season must sometimes be April, fair beyond fiction,
The inner crocus, enamel; the apple-trees
Fierce with fragrance and strength.   You must move among these
In the common lot.   Are you dogged by a minor friction?

When in at your window starlight is spilt
From the midnight sky and you, still watcher, see
The moon in silence pass each boundary,
The moon which never will acknowledge guilt,

When your two hands, fresh from their late employ,
Touch in the dark your lover's body, after;
When in the first hot sun climbs her clear laughter,
Do you meet the simplicity of joy?

And when the ambiguous bird in the dark meadow
Cries out an undecipherable message,
And utter stillness is the moment's presage
When there shall bend above you a chill shadow,

Then are you lonely only as all are lonely
Leaving the loved and known, or do you see
A small unnatural eternity
Shaped otherwise, and fashioned for you only?

April Asylum

I   They Were Showing a Film of Bermuda in Hammond II

The mad old women, bolted from April's weather,
Sit, in their morning rows, cautious, intent,
And Technicolor, like a sacrament,
Is raised to bless the lonely and together.

In the barred window ten o'clock puts free
Gilt on the potted lily; air outside
Stirs up the scent of the petalled plum-tree's tide
Boiling surf-white on the blue ether-sea.

Sheltered by iron, washed and dressed and fed,
Resistant to motion foreign as a wing,—
Before it moves the sea, behind it, spring,
This audience of docile sentient dead.

Repeating white on blue, the seascape screen
Crests, crashes, curdles;   on this dim locked beach
Neat sit the mad old women (cautious, each
Gray secret face raised quietly,) between.

II   A Thunderstorm Rose Back of The Building

The Lion-House, the Elephant-House, the Snakes, were Sunday wonder,
And "Zoo," echoes the mind;   but the childish fear was fun
And now along the adult horizon ruffles the muffled thunder.

The rain holds off.   In simple dark equality of plight
The similarities, though superficial, run:
(Peanuts subtracted, shirt-sleeves and drinking-fountains and delight,)

Hygiene; slant sun-made bars across cement; the sound of keys .
On rings; the terminology: Identity, Adult Female,
Although at feeding-time the kindly keeper calls "Louise!"

But where the lynx lay watchful on its gray fake treestub
And the hippo blew and floated monstrous in its stale
Small pool and up the piled rocks toiled the frowsy bear-cub

Lay jungle isolation like a blessing.   And never never
The thread that leads to distant nerves in tangled fever
Of thin tough pain, that leads to loves no rational knife can sever.

III   The Storm Cleared Rapidly

Over the dripping fruit-trees breaks the sky
Plum-blue to angel-blue,
The bird-calls shimmer, glittering-new
Curls for the visitor the gravel drive

Where, on the blazing grass, sits the wet granite,
Abadon's solid shelter,
The structure season shall not alter,
Housing the private and disastrous climate.

**IV   When the Patient Passed by, the Music Teacher
Was Practicing in the Open Window**

The weeping crabapple trails its pink tradition,
The plum shakes thickly white because of seed,
The algebra of grass recites its creed:
Green + soft × silent furious fission
= this breed.

The flute-notes fall contemplative and single,
Linked in a chain of never-more-nor-less,
Over the architectural happiness
The tufted tit-mouse, under the sun-hot shingle,
Constructed with success.

Above move clouds in current, underneath
Flow capable earthworms, functional and mute;
Black bloom on white, and gala as a wreath,
The notes in logic cluster: human breath
Counts clearly on the flute.

Only, on the purposeful path, obscene and frail,
Weaves weak from edge to edge the menaced stranger,
Opposing the cherry, the plum; the loose-mouthed Male,
Carrying as usual the empty and purposeless pail.
Alone, in danger.

Errant beneath the normal blossom's force,
Under the fragrance from their thousand throats,
Flanked by green blades, unarmed, without a course
Alone alone where fall without remorse
The deadly notes.

From *The Animal Inside*

Poems for My Cousin

for John

I   I Took My Cousin to Prettyboy Dam

I took my cousin to Prettyboy Dam.
A boxer was swimming for sticks, the ripples
Blew from the left, and beer cans glittered
Under the poison-ivy.

We talked of pelota; and how the tendrils of vines
Curl opposite ways in the opposite hemispheres.
My cousin was dying.   By this I mean
The rate of his disengagement was rapid.

There was a haze of heat, and August boys
Chunked rocks at a bottle that bobbed on the water.
The slow hours enclosed the flight of instants,
Melted the picnic-ice.

Everything he saw differently, and more clearly than I.
The joined dragonflies, the solid foam of the fall;
The thin haste of the ant at my foot,
And me, as I looked at him.

We were close beside each other, speaking of
Pelota, chaining cigarettes when the matches were gone.
But we saw different things, since one could not say
"Wait . . ."
Nor the other "Come . . ."

II   The Four Faces of My Cousin

My cousin had four faces.

One was the face which grimaced
In laughter or anger— mobile to danger,
Fun, or sudden love;

With the harrassed grain, and strains
Of wretched encounters, the thought
Of difficult heaven, and sudden love.

Made up of flaws, joys, private
Recall; of a benediction
Or so, and sudden love;

The second, was the blast of agony:
Contorted, it glared without sight
When the sheet was turned from the face

By familiar fingers.   It glared
Without rest under the harsh gesture
Of death, and the mouth was frantic for its breath.

The third, silent and silently watched
By the crucified man, had tiny pulses
Of light on its false tranquility—

The candle's mark.   It was a good mask,
Composed to duty and not unbeautiful
Below the poised and frilly inner lid.

But the gray-white was wrong, and the faint rouge
On a dead man's lips— (and the fingers
Curled stiffly, sharing the face's error.)

The fourth face of my cousin I have never
Seen.   This is the secret accurate intended
Face I must wait for.

III   Arrival of My Cousin

My cousin is arrived in
the green city of the dead.
It slopes, shapes itself
in hilly contours, and the summer light
lights all the white stones, crosses and angels of granite.

Thousands or tens of thousands
in the cool grass, under the flight
of birds, of shadows of birds; the shadow
of flight on sunny marble,
the bird-notes, bird-calls, dew-clear;
the blue and white sky is bent over my cousin
in the green city of the dead.

Traffic sweats and stalls on Oliver Street,
and Hargrove, Dolphin, Bethel Streets; the dirty bars
sweat, and the usual accidents in the Accident Rooms
are glazed by July, as are the gutters and the junk-man's
horse, jerked up the tar-soft mountain of July.
My cousin, however, is in the green city of the dead.

Not being of a primitive tribe
I speak in metaphor when I find my cousin,
cloud-free, granite-still, in
the green, bird-rich city, bounded
by the sweating streets, and the houses, and rooms,
and the people in streets, houses, rooms,
and their eyes.
By the body of Christ we ate, his absence
is evident:
But I speak of the token, the image
I was given for identity;
that word of flesh, like a name, a sound,
is what I speak of.

Infinitely not of the alley, the gutter, the traffic,
the sweating problem that walks
the pavement, sits in the room —
is the token, the word, the vanishing image of my cousin
under blue sky, white cloud, grass, bird-call, stone angel
in the green city of the dead.

Mr. Tantripp's Day

I   He Lit the Stove on a Cloudy Morning

The appalled heart at goosegray dawn,
As pale as ash, as old as lichen,
Goes down the stair in dogged flesh,
Beats coldly faint across the floor.
He takes both through the swinging door
Into the empty early kitchen.

The feather-sky sags on a mountain
Black-masked and eyeless as a mole —
He peers into the stove's round hole,
As chilly as a witch in hovel,
Then sends his diamond-hungry shovel
Into the swart slick shine of coal.

Now the heart kindles under its rib
For up, moon-size, the sun-disc goes
And burns the milky mist to blue
And purifies the dark to wonder.
He warms his hand where pulses under
The stove-lid purgatory's rose.

II   He Brought the Morning Paper from the Mailbox

Like lovers they move to this, like lovers in their trance,
Always toward each other; hot or cold,
Moon, neon, candle, sun; in every weather
That is not yet this weather,
Like lovers the killer and his to-be-killed
Choose, move, maneuver.   Like lovers in a dance

Still strangers, ignorantly still, advancing they use
The lesser intimacies: summer, a smashed wave,
Spaghetti instead of clams; an evening of laughter;
Select the kind of laughter;
Are afraid, but not of this. Like lovers, like dancers, they move
By choice, but draw nearer with each motion they choose.

And always while they fumble for change, whistle, sleep
Under each other's moon, choose the polka-dot tie,
The canary sweater, the days like veils dissolve
Fast fast and faster; they descry
Naked and steep the ultimate intimate sight:

The animal struggle, if only in the eyes' pain,
In turn flashes— like dying warlock fought—
Through serpent, fox, dove; to the last pose
The held submissive pose
Of forever, The sudden Escaped, the towering Caught.
They came to this by childhood corners and adolescent rain.

III   And After Dusk There Was a Show of Slides

The three looked, across the room, straight on
The Spanish mountains
Big and wild and dark.   Shone
Sunny haycocks; shone at their base
A field of wheat; acres of wheat
And vertical navy miles of mountain.

They breathed great air in that focused cheat
Of heavenly distance
When hairy darkness sat on wheat
Suddenly.   A black and giant fly

Blotted the haycocks and the gold
And set his fly legs across the distance:

Four balanced his hugeness, he briskly whetted
Two; like a toy
Of fear he stopped their breaths, he netted
Their breaths in the evil gauze of his wings
Flung over yellow wheat and cocks
Of hay.   Then he moved, like an ugly toy

And reason and faith ran.   Down dropped
The stupid breath.
The fragile monster started, stopped,
Pittered over a tiny mile of boulders
And black suddenly into blackness went,
Releasing Spain and screen and breath.

IV   With the Ancient Dog He Stepped Outside at Midnight

With him went the small black beast.
A dark wind shook the tamarisks
But could not blow the stars and moon about.

The dog had always vanished;
Never, once, come back unasked
Till now, tonight, quick as though menaced

By something in the humor
Of signals; the wind's tentative sound,
That watch-and-wait of eyes, stellar and lunar.

For close to the dog was a shape.
By the lit door love stood its ground.
The dog looked up in fear, in habit and hope.

At just this balance, beast and human,
The windy midnight spoke two words
Old and new for them to hear in common

Distinctly: *love* and *death*.
Then they moved separate, and the door
Shut them inside together for tonight at least.

And through the smallest hours
The still house like a brittle spar
Rode out the night among the jagged stars.

The Revolutionary

Certainly he knew her face well enough; had studied this
(perhaps this only), under the leafy stars in
the blown mountain midnight, with its sentry
the only waker, except herself and him.

Even by noon (clear as the dazzle
in his cupped palms, or the map he must draw
in red), her identity could scarcely escape him
who had held her on the cold ground asleep or awake.

Though it was by midnight in the hush of hope and silence
of stars that he studied the sleeper best — he her lover and guide.
His means were sparse, you understand: her face;
his map (in red); his sentry; and a handful of rifles.

After the map of her city broke to glory
(with her there, close, intimate as his blood),
worn with triumph, he fetched up in a proper bed.
Woke in the early sun, at a sound from her

and looked straight into hot whore eyes that stared
straight into his.   He could not fix the moment of change.
So he kept calling her by the old name he had used
for the face he had trusted under the confident stars.

The Eyes of Children at the Brink of the Sea's Grasp

The eyes of children at the brink of the sea's
Grasp, dilate, fix; their water-sculpted hair
Models their heads; crouching a little they stare
In motionless ecstacy of panic
As the upreared load, tilting, tilting titanic
Pitches and shocks them in a rainbow crash
And is upon them in a cat's flash
Before the nearest shrieks and flees.
Most true terror carries them high to us
Up sand as white and dry as safety— thereafter
Gooseflesh and shudders rack them to drunken laughter,
They reel, self-conscious, pantomiming . . .
But presently sober, cautious down the shining
Dark slope of invitation, outward, to the prize
Of shaping danger they go— and widen their eyes
Innocent and voluptuous.

We Met in the City

We met in the city.

Love, if the earth were to my teeth
I would say this, so
listen.
We met in the city.

Who held it, who assaulted, we could not be sure
ever.
Spies passed as children and heroism
mined it like tunnels.
We believed
it had changed hands often — should we fear
besiegers or besieged?
Certainly the peril was extreme.

It was most often night — the bone stones
whitened like echoes of the moon;
the shadows geometric and significant
hid opportunities or only a passerby.
The barbarous birds with cries
like tin torn
swept close; moon and dark
masked the zebra rocks and our own fingers.

For all the patrols and wire, a room blazed
often in a ripped building like a secret
mysterious and blatant: music, voices,
and under the music, laughter.
But the barricades were shifted
constantly and names and addresses were false.

Every so often a dawn
wide and solemn and silent, melted the stones
with almost lemon light and absolute stillness. One
lasted for hours once; and once a noon
exploded and folded the night in sun
a dust of summer grass and an image of sheep.

The noon was too circular and told us nothing—
or so we thought at the time.
But the rare dawns altered all angles always
and a map appeared, starry and strange
and familiar and frightening.
I saw it on your body— veins and angles
features and colors the same but different;
after dawn came night and the great birds ripped by.

The three-legged cat paused, cocked her
mouse at us, both zebra-striped;
the hunch-backed tart greeted us gently.
What made us think the city's fall
this time would be
to the final conqueror?

We knew it.

We never failed to find each other.
By luck by love by some grotesque device,
can you believe it? in those acres of rubble
those meadows of midnight those moonlight stridencies—
later, or sooner,
bearing new marks or chinking gold like thieves,
under the wings' rush, in the zebra shadows,

we saw the angles, nerves, blood, veins,
glance, gesture,
the shorthand code, the message of each other.
O it was worthwhile!

That city.
When moonlight filled it like a cistern
it gave back some reflection —
liquid, moving, distorted —

a chart or map or an equation
in its degenerate wavering glass.

If the earth were to my teeth
I would say
so:
we met in the city.
But we met.

The Three Children

Else has blown away on the east wind, Richard went away with the wind
        from the west.
Hilary was taken by the wind from the true north.
Still the south wind is here today but the children are gone. Like witches or
        fairytale sons
They came in a three.   Like roses or leaves
Or laughter they were gusty.   The roses moved and the clear leaves,
        the weather was sunny.
The turn is warm today and the leaves limpid and the roses running.

Else turned somersaults on the granite flags, she had had two years to learn
        whatever she had learned.
She loved fear and a great black dog knocked her down and licked her
        rumpled face and she screamed for joy.
She waltzed on the steep steps and languished through the bannisters.
Richard had thirteen more months, and the plans of monsters
Much on his mind.   Richard hoped all things while the tricky earth turned
        him over and over.
He was benevolent and wept only at wickedness.

And the wind moved his hair and the leaves and roses around him. Hilary
        had a secret or two
Too heavy to touch.   He dazzled and dawdled
And understood, with reluctance, thorns and chlorophyll and frost in roses
        and leaves and winds.
He has gone to school to learn simpler things.
The kind gardens of kindergarten have opened their mazes of reassurance to
        Richard and Else.
Here the wind made the summer of leaves and roses

Blow flying and running about them.   The black dog bounded, the
    thunder moved and the hours blew round.
On the tomato-sprayer the cross-bones and skull
Behind the pail in the shed smiled at them, but briefly.   In the peaked
    house hung the still bell
And the crayon-man figure was pinned
To sticks and the flames like roses blew in a wind's ghost. The children in
    secret wonder
Watched the faces that watched them.

This is one summer and not another. Goodbye, three children never to be
    seen again. *We will come back*
They said, but they will not.   They will go so quietly, so completely.
Next summer three strangers whose names were handed like torches from
    the three that went on the north,
East, west winds, from the three who could not stay and went forever
At no moment with no gesture, irrecoverable as a single petal or a green
    ghost flying, who went

Where?

Instances of Communication

Almost nothing concerns me but communication.
How strange: Up the Orinoco, once, far
up the Orinoco after jungle miles, great flowerheads
looping the treecrests, log-crocodiles, crocodile-logs, bob-haired
Indians naked in praus: a small hot town and in an upper dining-room
plashed at by a fountain, cooled by fans, guardian of a menu the size of a
        baby,
speaking six languages with seven capital cities behind his eyes, a head-
        waiter,
a man, who said without hope, *"And when does your ship sail"*? And no
        one said to him, *"What are you doing here?"*

In the hall of the inn at Mont Serrat I came out of my room and
"Stand back, stand back!" cried the criada in her softest Spanish, *"the
        bride —*
the bride is coming!"   out of her room, down the hall, down to the steps
on her way to the church, to the groom.   She was pale and dark; she
        clouded
the carpet with the mist of her train, she moved by me but turned and bent
        and caught
my fingerbones seeing me like fate, watching the three of her, the old tall
        childhood girl,
the darkly seen half-a-thing, and the white bride lost on the point of love,
        and *"Buenas*
o buenas tardes!"   she called into my ear, she crushed my fingers and
        laughed with panic
into my widened eyes and went proudly on whispering over the hall runner.

I drove five madwomen down a roaring redhot turnpike in a July
noon; the one behind me had a fur ragged coat gathered about her in that
	furnace;
she reached in the horrid insides of a purse and offered me a chocolate,
	liquid
and appalling.   *"Look!   Look!   A bird!"* I cried and flung it over the side,
and munched my empty jaws as she turned back, and cried *"How good!"*
And while the others hummed and cursed, and watched simply, suddenly
	she put
her lips— behind me— to my ear and soft as liquid chocolate came purling
the obscene abuse.   *"Hush, hush, Laura, hush,"* said the nurse; *"the
	nice lady
likes you!"*   Laura did not believe so, and went on slowly, softly, with O such
	misery of hate.

In frosty Philadelphia the freighter lay and loaded in the Sunday
ice. The great cranes swung, the huge nets grabbed and everything echoed
	from cold:
docks, warehouses, freightrails, ships' prows; everything clicked and echoed;
but it was possible to go down the long cold docks over the strange dark
	street under
the dim sky into a cold great warehouse Sunday still, up still cold stairs,
	along
a dark dim cold thin hall through a brown door into a small square room
	with lit
peaky candles and kneeling take— cool, slick, thin, little larger than a
	quarter—
God's blood and body charged with its speech.

The Animals

At night, alone, the animals came and shone.
The darkness whirled but silent shone the animals:
the lion the man the calf the eagle saying
Sanctus which was and is and is to come.

The sleeper watched the people at the waterless wilderness' edge;
The wilderness was made of granite, of thorn, of death,
It was the goat which lightened the people praying.
The goat went out with sin on its sunken head.

On the sleeper's midnight and the smaller after-hours
From above below elsewhere there shone the animals
Through the circular dark;   the cock appeared in light
Crying three times, for tears for tears for tears.

High in the frozen tree the sparrow sat.   At three o'clock
The luminous thunder of his fall shook the earth.
The somber serpent looped its coils to write
In scales the slow snake-music of the red ripe globe.

To the sleeper, alone, the animals came and shone,
The darkness whirled but silent shone the animals.
Just before dawn the dove flew out of the dark
Flying with green in her beak; the dove also had come.

Yellow

Yellow became alive.
Materialization took place.
First logically with lemons,
then fresh butter.
Also a chair-leg.
After that it appeared
to carve the curve of clouds
and, as sun, shatter them.
The stars grew yellower
yellow whirls on wheels on whirls
leaves flew yellow
the corn sprang
yellow and the crows
winged with a yellow nimbus.
Finally his face
had brilliant yellow
in its grain.
Outside the madhouse hung the yellow sun.

Arrival of Rain

At midnight
it began to rain.

The sound of rain everywhere
fills my hollow ear.
The dry weeks round I was not thinking of that sound—
two sounds, the sound
of falling and the sound of drinking—
now here.

Dusty root darkens and the stubble sharpening
its cruel shafts, softens;
my hollow ear harkening
hears stubble green and moisten,
all drinking all darkening;
the liquid beaded sigh
of sound, two sounds
everywhere and here
in the hollow avid ear.

All need is dry.
Rain is the metaphor.

The Sea Fog

It was sudden.
That slightly heaving hotel, from a folder,
was there one instant: through the glass a bloodorange ball
just diving, a pure blue desert of dusk
on the other horizon; a motion, the symbol of seas;
music, and drinks, and the self-conscious apparel,
the relative facets, of steward and poster, and sun-disc
just hidden.

The ship spoke
with a minotaur sound from around and under
and we raised our eyes: but the sea was gone:
sub-sun, the peel of moon, the plausible shift
of dunes of water, our precious image of movement—
gone, gone, clean gone. The fog was at the pane.
No shore behind us; ahead in the breathy drift
no port.

Supported
by shore and port, now we had neither.
There was only here. The ship was here
in the fog. The ship roared and the fog blotted
us into itself and whirled into its rifts,
and the sealess skyless fear—and there was fear—
had nothing to do with sinking—at least, not
into water.

Worse:
when we went below, at the familiar turn
a bulkhead reared instead, metal and huge—
and trapped, we turned from that hulk and hastened
through stranger stairs and came from a different angle
to a cabin stiller and smaller though none of its objects had moved.
But the mirror stirred like fog when we looked for the fastened face.

We crept
through fog all night but it closed behind us:
around and very close above:
Only below the black the self-lit fishes
passed ignorantly among the racks of wrecks
and all the water held its tongue and gave
no password; and so sealed in our motionless passage
we slept.

The bell
for the bulkhead doors to open, woke us.
Everything had been reconnected: sun to the sea,
ship to the sun, smiles to our lips, and our names related
to our eyes. Who could—in that brassy blue—
have stillness to harbour the memory
of being relative to nothing; isolated;
responsible?

From *The Shade-Seller*

The Shade-Seller

for A. R. Ammons

"Sombra?"
he asked us from his little booth. And shade
we bought to leave our car in.

By noon
the sand was a mealy fire; we crossed by planks
to the Revolcadero sea.

One day
we were later and hotter; and he peered out
and "No hay sombra!" he told us.

That day
when we came back to our metal box, frightened
we breathed for a terrible instant

the air
fiery and loud of the hooked fish.
Quick! Quick! Our silver key!

Sometimes
now I dream of the shade-seller; from his dark
he leans, and "sombra . . ." I tell him.

There is
candescent sand and a great noise of heat
and it is I who speak that word

heavy
and wide and green. O may he never
answer my one with three.

The Crabracers

Suddenly, the music is mute; all the keys
lock up their notes that divided the sinuous palmfronds.
Sixty chairs go back with a mingled metal sound;
and drinks in hand all are off to the races.

The crabs are under a bowl with a giant bulb —
very hot, very bright — and are not apt to balk.
The bowl is the center of a generous circle in chalk,
and a circle of faces is a wheel with the crabs as its hub.

Then the bowl goes up, and the bets; and the crabs go.
On the strange concrete, springy under the cheers,
hard-shelled, bow-legged, in a wandering veer.
The motionless, dart sidewise; the most rapid, slows

a sinful inch from the chalk. Screams, and new highs.
A lumbering lurker puts a pincer over.
A hundred yards away the salt sea says, I cover
the sand, the sand says, I return my prizes.

The Caribbean is near to the crabs, and the sand is closer,
pitted with holes in its heaved dryness; thick
with viscous moonlight where the edges are slick.
The crabs are back in the bowl, and the bulb is hotter.

Money has changed hands. The reassured people,
closer, brighter, are ready for the second race.
The tide times the people, as the bowl is raised,
hub of a circle beyond the crabs' circle.

Bush

for Ricky

It is the sound of lions lapping.
They drink themselves
from the gold shapes that waver
and grow shallower.

Blue peels itself in the water-
hole; it is the sun coming.
Crouched, the lions meet
their matches at the surface.

The foxy jackals are far off
but the vultures cloud the flat treetop;
the drum of the zebra's body
is lined with red sunrise.

The jackals and vultures are waiting
for what happened under the moon.
The lions are through with it; they
lift their dripping chins and look ahead.

It is six o'clock on Christmas morning.
Now the lions have stopped lapping
the bush makes no sound
the vultures shift, but without sound.

The day is perfectly seamless.
Slowly the lions move like pistons past the dry grasses;
the jackals do not move yet;
the vultures show patience.

The lions pass a thornbush and melt.
Though the whole day is unbroken
the passage of the sun will represent heaven;
the bones will represent time.

My Small Aunt

       died in a dust of lions; her Africa
was secret as her body and arrived
like the biblical robber by night, by darkest night;
that night, however, was the cinema's:
where there before her, high and bright, and wide
as love, it stretched its radiant sinister light.
And by the foreground clump of pampas grass
shone the pride.

She knew it all before she saw it all.
Light-hearted as a warrior come home
she absolved its horrors: the bald-neck buzzards,
carrion-content; and in the waterhole
the gross great pigs that float their eyes on scum;
the cough, the red snatched meal, the hot-breathed hazard;
in what sense the pride goeth before the fall —
the hunted one.

Was she the hunter or the hunted? Both.
At home, the click and tick of cup and clock
failed to falter in any changes. Hunted
by pain, and tireless hunter of the moth,
she turned no key within a useless lock.
No nephew, nay, no friend, went disappointed.
But in her sun slept lions, chockablock
with blood and sloth.

She queued for her ticket in the stale winter street,
and, step for step, the mean wind cried like a ghoul
in her ear and flourished its trash and her blue eye wept.

But closer and close, the aromatic heat
and the flat trees; and like a homing soul
she met the spaces the hot grasses kept
and met the motion of four soundless feet:
the paced prowl.

Hunted or hunter. Too brave to be sad,
the fear of pity fixed her like a stare.
Sharp starry hunters, luminous orions
whirled in her sleep. Taking her cup in bed
she drank unsweetened courage black and clear.
In their gold ruffs waited the shining lions,
violent and sunny lords who never had
pity or fear.

The Class

The small black blobs on the beach are the heads
of children.   Defectives:
the imbeciles could not come, and the morons
have graduated to lives.
Five sit under the sun at the tide's edge.

Everything moves: Like a motion of silence a sailboat
goes on the sea's brilliant shiver;
the glittery palms make the sound of raining,
clouds change shape, waves curl over.
The five stay still as five struck in one pose.

They are out for an outing in the great free air:
they face the Caribbean;
the air will not bear them up, nor the sea
nor the sand grow an herb to heal,
nor the thick white clouds transport them elsewhere.

This is no lesson the voice gives.
They listen, listen in a secret school,
their faces lifted: conscienceless, on their skin
the tongue of the tide says, *Cool* . . .
and in glazed brightness the sun says, *Live* . . .

An Absence of Slaves

The Greek guide
said:
"I want you to remember one thing."
With her deep voice and curly
hair
and small shocked shoes, she said,
"This is our pride:

this was free
labor:
free men built this Par-
thenon. Athenians
left fold and press and field
and harbor:
gave no slavery."

The sun broke
on glorious stone, ripped from the dark
quarry;   she said: "The city
sent a slave
to each man's yoke,
oil press and furrow,
to free for toil the free Greek:

the free raised these!" she cried
to the blue sky and honey-
veined columns.   "This is
no pyramid."   And I saw
the loins and wrists
and bones and tendons of those disprized
who in absence reared the great frieze.

Return from Delphi

Coming from Delphi in the rain we met a country funeral.

At Delphi last night traveling the wastes of sky, a bare
round moon went and the stream rushed in the absolute
pause of time, the cold furious sacred stream
away below; the big black mountain
mounted in blackness the milky air.
Oracle in no lair.

"A procession?" Our bus slows in the narrow road,
                                            rain-pricked,
jostling lightly. We look through open windows.

A brilliant morning told us another story:
the water, hill and air being bright; and the god's slope
tumbled with honey-veined milky stone, grew flowers;
his columns stood on stone that allows
yellow blossoms to grow.

"A funeral?" "Yes!" A purple cloth. Then children — boys,
no girls; one holding a cupped flame on a pole, they go;
then the priest's black billows; then on six shoulders
                                            the burden.

Fine as needles the rain began at eleven; in and out
of the holes in the Athenian Treasury the sparrows flew.
Was our magnet columns and blocks? Nonsense! We know,
All of us, what: Apollo.

She is not closed away. She is old.
                    She is lying in cold spring flowers
close to our astonished faces; see how we stare.
On her stonestill breast her rainy hands are crossed;
powerful nose, still lips, she is yellow like stone.

One thing brought us to Delphi, the scent of the god;
in the cypress thrust, in the rocks where
we climbed; in our care. In our care.

The feet go past to the earth. The vines like snakes
rear from the earth and petals of almond blow
and alight on the earth. We in our leather seats,
prim animals with the knowledge of death in our eyes,
exchange quick glances of complicity.

The rites, the gifts; it all meant Show
a sign. Speak now.

Beaded with rain in the dusk they are gone.
                    The flame, the tilted
cross, the homage of bearing, the honor of flow-
ers, have turned an old woman toward spring, in the dust
of the olives, in the soil of the vines; the honor was
                    for the passage,
that part of the gesture—the columns broken, unbroken.

For the confrontation of where, of how.

The stone said so.

The quick was the god's gesture — unpredictable,
precious, final. That light on stone, horses that rear
to stone, stone eyes, stone wind, meant one point: the man,
the god, the question. In isolation, the earth's shift,
the light darkening. Old woman, yellow like stone, yours
was no delphic answer. Far and fair
on our dark, silent Athens is there.

The Sparrows at Delphi

Sparrows
are in the Treasury of Athens, in the holes
between the pale honey-veined blocks;
the sparrows are whole
and have not been
restored.
Not even a beak or a wing-tip is
chipped.
To the hollow spaces of the empty Athe-
nian Treasury
on the god's slope at Delphi
go in the sparrows.

The Parthenon Frieze

On the Thessalian plain
almond and apricot still
in this sun stir from,
the grasses lift after,
the galloping of the invisible horses,
the wind of their passage
the great thighs' rush
the kindling manes
the hooves that sprang

to stone.

The Lovers

The lovers lie in the shelter of night, the lovers
lie in each other's arms in night's crux:
the clock stopped and stars still and fire
unlit, in each other's arms lie the lovers.

Still clock and stopped stars are not true:
cold dust blows from the stars, cold iron roars
through space, time ticks trapped in the two
lovers' wrists.   False, stopped clock and still stars.

On the cold hearth, to kindle the lovers' fire,
stuffed under logs lie inky rage and retribution;
on a nail on the wall, stretched arms and folded feet
hang and motionlessly reproduce an execution.

Here the stars make no sound, there is no wind, no clock.
Once an animal cried out in the tall cold meadow
grass, beyond the glass cried out, addressing owl or fox.
Who will stay the lovers in their single shadow?

The lovers lie in the shelter of their deaths;
though they move, now, to part, it is a feint at most:
who were two have died, and are safe in a single breath:
they are discovered, found with all the lost.

In the Crevice of Time

for Elliott Coleman

The bison, or tiger, or whatever beast
hunting or hunted, and the twiggy hunter
with legs and spear, in the still caves of Spain
wore out the million rains of summer
and the mean mists of winter:
the frightening motion of the hunter-priest

who straight in the instant between blood and breath
saw frozen there not shank or horn or hide
but an arrangement of these by him, and he himself
there with them, watched by himself inside
the terrible functionless whole
in an offering strange as some new kind of death.

The thick gross early form that made a grave
said in one gesture, "neither bird nor leaf."
The news no animal need bear was out:
the knowledge of death, and time the wicked thief,
and the prompt monster of foreseeable grief:
it was the tentative gesture that he gave.

Our hulking confrère scraping the wall,
piling the dust over the motionless face:
in the abyss of time how he is close,
his art an act of faith, his grave
an act of art: for all,
for all, a celebration and a burial.

Notes from a Lenten Bar

I know that my redeemer liveth because
the pebble-eyed gent with the briefcase
two tables down has called him by name
3 times in 2 and 3/4 minutes;
and because
the guys on my right are liquid with the health
of victorious Immaculate Conception, 46 to 98;
and because
after the last of my supper, I learn once more
as I rise to 1403
there is nothing between the 12th and the 14th floor.

The Terrible Naive

sleepwalk, feed
birdseed to kittens,
dislike arithmetic of
courtesy;

omnipotently shrewd
will whistle
in mirrors; will wrestle,
but only after

securely lashing
your wrists with
their tough
vulnerability;

execute ambushes
with un-
loaded guns, but when
they cry

"I die! I die!"
the dark flood
is your
blood.

Destinations

Home is mysterious: a place to die, a place to breed;
a rock, a streambed, a burrow. From far far far
a deadly magnet: violent unarguable rapid need.

The wastes of waters, the printless wastes of air, prepare
for them death, failure: but never death of destination—
the thread snapped off in the labyrinth, the shifting of a star.

From the Brazilian water-pastures, in her homing passion
the green turtle travels fourteen hundred miles to find
(with tiny water-level eye) Ascension Island reared above her motion.

Eels. No eel in the west world but is reminded
in autumn of Sargasso; to its weeds and washes comes in spring
to breed, and to die; the elvers will return to do in kind.

The Manx shearwater (monogamous as a wolf) flying
back back to his unidentifiable cliffy burrow; the albatross,
the salmon; need I labor the point in fur, fin, wing?

The point is established. But if I swim, I sink, if I fly, I fall.
How do I then know that over the terrible distance where you are, I must
       arrive?
The point is established. But the how, the how is not established at all.

But there is a question below the question of how I contrive
finally to reach you through the disasters of my weather.
I must come, and I come; so I accede, prevail, arrive.

But we are tricked. O most fortunate fin and feather,
fortunate voyagers, come where you had to go.
But it turns out that this was a shelter, a shelter we leave together
for elsewhere: and the shadows pulsing say *night* and the short wind says
   snow.

The Planet

for Erlend

From the center of the Sea of Tranquility—
a dry sea and a grainy—
see shining on the air
of that stretched night, a planet.

See it as serene and bright, very bright,
a far fair neighbor;
conceive what might be there
after the furious spaces.

Green fields, green fields,
oceans of grasses, breakers of daisies;
shadows on those fields,
vast and travelling,

the clouds' shadows.
And something smaller:
in the green grass, lovers in each other's
arms, still, in the grass.

The clouds will water the fields
the stream run shining
to the sea's motion; the sea shining
as the clouds travel and shine,

so shine the daisies, as
the light in the seas
of the lovers' eyes. The innocent planet
far and simple, simple because far:

with lovers, and fields for flowers,
and a blue sky carrying clouds;
and water, water: the innocent planet,
shining and shining

Gentle Reader

Late in the night when I should be asleep
under the city stars in a small room
I read a poet. A poet: not
a versifier. Not a hot-shot
ethic-monger, laying about
him; not a diary of lying
about in cruel cruel beds, crying.
A poet, dangerous and steep.

O God, it peels me, juices me like a press;
this poetry drinks me, eats me, gut and marrow
until I exist in its jester's sorrow,
until my juices feed a savage sight
that runs along the lines, bright
as beasts' eyes. The rubble splays to dust:
city, book, bed, leaving my ear's lust
saying like Molly, yes, yes, yes, O yes.

From *The Chinese Insomniacs*

The Chinese Insomniacs

It is good to know
the Chinese insomniacs.
How, in 495 A.D.,
in 500 B.C.,
the moon shining, and the pine-
trees shining back
at it, a poet had to walk
to the window.

It is companionable
to remember my fellow
who was unable to sleep
because of a sorrow, or not;
who had to watch
for the wind
to stir night flowers in the garden
instead of making the deep journey.

They live nine hun-
dred years apart,
and turn, and turn, restless.
She says her sleeve is wet
with tears; he says something difficult
to forget, like
music counts the heartbeat.

A date is only a mark
on paper—it has little to do
with what is long.
It is good to have their company
tonight: a lady, awake
until birdsong;
a gentleman who made
poems later out of frag-
ments of the dark.

Mr. Mahoney

Illicitly, Mr. Mahoney roams.
They have him in a room, but it is not his.
Though he has become confused, it is not in this.
Mr. Mahoney cannot find his room.

A young blond nurse gentles him by the elbow.
I hear her again in the hall: "Mr. Mahoney,
this isn't your room. Let's go back and see
if you've brushed your teeth. Yours is 820."

Why brushing his teeth is the lure, I cannot say.
Does he prize it so? She darts on white feet
to spear him from strange doors; I hear her repeat
with an angel's patience, "Yours is down *this* way."

But 820 is a swamp, a blasted heath.
A dozen times returned, he knows it is wrong.
There is a room in which he does belong.
He has been to 820; he has brushed his teeth.

Before his biopsy, the harried nurses attest,
Mr. Mahoney was tractable in 820,
though very old and brown. He will have to go;
this is not the hall, not the building for his quest.

Tranquilized, Mr. Mahoney still eludes.
At 2 A.M. in my dark 283
the wide door cracks, and sudden and silently
Mr. Mahoney's nutty face obtrudes.

It is gently snatched back by someone behind it.
"That is someone *else's* room. Yours is this way,
Mr. Mahoney." He could not possibly stay.
He is gone by noon. He did not have time to find it.

Pondicherry Blues

Mrs. Pondicherry was/ fat and mean,
she had four/ pug/ dogs and a limousine
black/ as West Virginia coal;
and she troubled herself about her soul,
yes, she surely was concerned/ about her soul.

Father O'Hare was thin as a steeple,
the poor and the lonely were his passion and his people.
Pondicherry would ask/ that man to come to dinner
and talk/ to him/ about The Sinner.
And Father O'Hare got very/ very/ tired of Mrs. Pondicherry,
he got raw-/ bone/ tired of Pondicherry.

She changed her will like/ she changed her furs
cause she surely did know that they both were hers,
and she drove that man beside himself
with her wills/ and her pelts/ and her pugs/ and her pelf,
she drove him purely beside himself.

One day she was sitting on her velvet seat
her mink/ round her shoulders and her footstool for her feet
and a cushion for/ each/ pug;
and her heart gave a leap and she fell on the rug,
she fell/ right/ down/ on her big/ red/ rug.

They put her into/ bed and called Father O'Hare
but he couldn't get there and he couldn't get there
and she lay on her bed for a/ solid/ hour

and she didn't say a word cause she didn't own the power,
didn't own the power to say/ a single word.

Her mind was thin and cold as a hag
in her eyes was a beggar with a/ bowl and a rag,
and her ears/ heard/ a cold/ wind start
to blow the trash round the alleys of her heart,
to blow/ cold/ trash round the gutters of her heart.

But Father O'Hare he was/ serving the poor,
he never reached the house and he never crossed the door
till she closed her eyes and/ she stopped her breath
in the lonesome/ slum/ of death
that dark/ trashy/ street of/ death.

The Gondolas

All night the gondolas knock
knock softly lightly like a hand
secure in its message. Under the windows, down
in the dark
the black gondolas knock softly.

Noon hushes the hand.
Pigeons flung into the sun they darken
glitter, break into fragments, fall
to fold their flight and stepping, stop;
the lion stares, all stars and wings, but stands;
the sumptuous banners move out and up
in the wind's hand;
flowing palazzi's peaks
shimmer and stream, their colors melt and flow
the bridges arching down melt under prows
the clouds confuse them as the bells
melt all their metal in the summer air.

At night the echoes echo echoes:
now you hear
the slight slap, ageless,
below sealed doors,
the soft quasi-silent slap
of water on the dank green sides of stone,
on the soft brilliant moss of footless steps.
Down black still ways palazzi go, deeper
than last night, into sleep.

The lights' cold broken flash
catches an orange peel, a stir of dark:
the soft slight slap jostles the gondolas
the black long empty gondolas
stir, knocking lightly
with a light hollow knocking
like a confident hand.

The Dream Habitués

Odd we've never met there,
spending all that time.
But then, it's a big country.

Erratic, too, as to lighting and climate.
Will it be crowded,
or the reverse? Tiresome, as to entry?

Yet I keep going back. God knows how often,
if I added up. Which means
I ought to know a fair-

sized group. But the people move about so.
And total strangers accost you,
looking familiar.

And the transportation!
Take you off to see a ruin, or cave,
and forget you. That's at its worst.

Yes, I've had incidents
curl the hair on my head.
But then at its best

how marvelous . . . I had a dance
there once more like, well,
swimming? or flying? No. Nothing I'd learned.

A couple of bad experiences.
And one doesn't know,
so to speak, which way to turn,

But then that can happen —
or something almost like it —
in any city. The closest shave.

And, if one wishes,
one can always wake.
Or, so far, I have.

Phrases in Common Use

I have brought the phrase book. The rain has stopped,
wind makes the grass glitter and wink,
It is early: e cedo. And early in spring, too,
brown lambs and almond buds. The sun like a flute
stands the bare black vines on their tails, the snaky vines rise up

forked, black and bare.
My love, it is early. The bell bangs from the convent
on top of the hill
(all these Portuguese hills are blue as bluebells),
hear the flat sweet bang over the winking green:
e cedo.

Last night the phrases fell with the drops
in a dream of rain: the Phrases in Common Use.
A que distancia? Well, rather far. *Sao
horas de partir?* Not yet. Not really yet.
E tarde. And, if late and rainy,
then, *tenhio frio: I am cold.*
This is too hard: *I have bought
only a few things during my stay.*
And useful, but almost equally difficult: *I shall be glad
to help you, accompany you, invite you.*
And which to choose: *A culpa, (nao) foi minha:
It was (was not) my fault.*

This morning I understand that I do not need
to remember how to say any of that;

it is for later. And I have not yet learned to say
brown lambs, or *almonds.*
E cedo: it is early. Feel the sun.
Air moves the grass and drops flash in its green tangles,
the two mimosas blaze like a brace of angels.
E cedo: it is early. Venha ca: come here
Prometo-lhe: I promise you.

Tears

Tears leave no mark on the soil
or pavement; certainly not in sand
or in any known rain forest;
never a mark on stone.
One would think that no one in Persepolis
or Ur ever wept.

You would assume that, like Alice,
we would all be swimming, buffeted
in a tide of tears.
But they disappear. Their heat goes.
Yet the globe is salt
with that savor.

The animals want no part in this.
The hare both screams and weeps
at her death, one poet says.
The stag, at death, rolls round drops
down his muzzle; but he is in
Shakespeare's forest.

These cases are mythically rare.
No, it is the human being who persistently
weeps; in some countries, openly, in others, not.
Children who, even when frightened, weep most hopefully;
women, licensed weepers.
Men, in secret, or childishly; or nobly.

Could tears not make a sea of their mass?
It could be salt and wild enough;
it could rouse storms and sink ships,
erode, erode its shores:
tears of rage, of love, of torture,
of loss. Of loss.

Must we see the future
in order to weep? Or the past?
Is that why the animals
refuse to shed tears?
But what of the present, the tears of the present?
The awful relief, like breath

after strangling? The generosity
of the verb "to shed"?
They are a classless possession
yet are not found in the museum
of even our greatest city.
Sometimes what was human, turns
into an animal, dry-eyed.

Rainy Night at the Writers' Colony

Dead poets stalk the air,
stride through tall rain and peer
through wet panes where
we sleep, or do not, here.

I know the names of some
and can say what they said.
What do we say worth the while
of the ears of the dead?

I know who shook marred
fruit of difficult bough
and from the rank discard
salvaged enough.

The rain stops; at two
the moon comes clear.
What they did, we know.
It is we who are here.

Naked under their eye,
we — honest, grave, greedy,
pedant, fool — lie
with what we make of need.

The Monosyllable

One day
she fell
in love with its
heft and speed.
Tough, lean,

fast as light
slow
as a cloud.
It took care
of rain, short

noon, long dark.
It had rough kin;
did not stall.
With it, she said,
I may,

if I can,
sleep; since I must,
die.
Some say,
rise.

Border

That country has never been her enemy.
She speaks its language, it uses hers freely.
Its flags make her heart lurch
and its music is indistinguishable from her desire.
Certainly, there are forests
only the crowns of which she has seen,
and a great river that keeps them green.

It is no reflection upon her that
she lacks a visa.
There is no visa.
Ambassadors come constantly
with a great variety of gifts;
blossoms and leaves.

She lives at its frontier, goes and comes
along its border, touching the great seal
with her hand.
The king comes over to sleep with her.

Short Views in Africa

I

The elephant
comes past the Visitor two feet away,
watched through the blind's
chink. His shoulder strides,
he places a solemn foot,
then another.
The tufted tail goes by.

High up, at night, the Visitor sees
the herd come out:
singly, in moonlight, from the bush, the trees;
by twos; in a file of huge three;
scoop mud, blow, breathe. 103 elephants.

The Visitor
is healed by elephants,
pretends they will stay; falls asleep
kneeling at the sill. At four
the Visitor's eyes open:
the herd, rocking and shifting,
blowing, putting plashy feet,
is preparing to leave.
When the sun wakes her
they are somewhere else.

II

The best surprise is death.
She dreaded this

but it fits lightly. Even the frantic spurt,
ripped flank, snapped neck
settle so easily to: rock,
gold grass, stubble, bones, bones.

Everywhere, bones.
Simple, the bones of beasts.
This is the short view,
like a cut nerve — peace.
The bones are everywhere like grace
in the early sun.

III

The long, warped triangle
of the giraffe's pretty face,
the paintbrush lashes, the roving head
over the thornbush cruise, shy and leafy.
This air is pure with the ignorance of death.

Cat-lax the lion blinks
in noon's thin shade.
Lioness raises her head, stares,
lowers it; in a heap
the cubs are burrowed, dazed
with red food.

The skeletons inside the warm fur
go by paces, by springs, by stalks,

to their final sun;
to light, wind, grass.
Knowledgeable,
the Visitor watches the lions.

IV

In Olduvai are the bones
that block the way to ignorance.
Which bones, which minute first
looked on death and said, "That
belongs to me." Then said, then later said,
". . . belongs to what I love."

The Visitor can imagine herself—
imagines herself—
into the short sunny view;
bones unrelated, messageless,
the million bones benevolently whitening,
crying nothing
but hunger and motion;
not secretive of the permanent desire; not
saying
Mary Ann Kelly, Beloved.
Xenophon lies here.
I was Hannah.

V

Well. Bless the giraffe,
the elephant, the lioness, the short
blessed view.

Kneel at the window.
Wait under the thorntree
for the sun. Go away
carrying your difference, you cannot leave it.
Say, Not God
himself would dare to lay it on you without
relief.
Tell your secret bones: Wait.

A Motel in Troy, New York

A shadow falls
on our cribbage. The motel window
is a glass wall down to grass.

A huge swan
is looking in: cumulus-cloud body,
thunder-cloud dirty neck

that hoists the painted face
coral and black. Inky eyes
peer at our lives.

It cannot clean its strong
snake neck. It stands
squat on its yellow webs

splayed to hold
scarcely up the heavy
feathered dazzle.

All of us stare. Then
in a lurch it turns
and waddles rocking,

presses the stubble to the tip
of the blue pond. Sets sail
in one pure motion

and is received by distance.
That crucial soiled snake neck
arched to a white high curve

received by distance
and the shadowy girl
across the water.

Trial Run

But I think that things are the same with many
today as they were in Noah's time, when he built
the Ark of planks and timbers: for none of the
workmen and carpenters who fashioned it were
saved . . .

Piers Ploughman

They saw it take the water—the finished Ark,
after that long ridiculous procession:
the question-mark giraffe, the elephant
waving its ears, placing its plushy foot;
the loose-lip goat burning its yellow eye.
It floated, worthy, tight as you could ask.

Even where they watched, clotted on the top rocks,
would be a shining welter in, say, another hour:
not one green thing to clutch at as they went,
but water down upon them, up, to catch them—
the liquid howl of chaos, carrying
that tight right bark with all its procreant freight.

On the last sunny day (caulking the seams,
the green trees like a fleet of anchored clouds
above them; the crucial frame, the smell of shavings,
and the honor of accuracy, under the sweet blue
sky, paling, paling), they had understood
the only part of them to go would be the job.

It seemed unfair, but no more arguable
than the waters and the rough great wind.
And one, at least, just as the first cold hand
of water took his ankle, had a thought
that he would rather see her ride there, his,
still faintly seen, than, rocking in her hold

stand docile on commissioned planks.
She would bear it out, he knew, with bleat
and grunt and howl, and—doves being doves—
one might find out a green tree or its leaf.
In any case, it rode so as to argue
some future fortune for a carpenter.

Food

A woman of the more primitive tribes
of Eskimo, concerned with nourishment,
cooked with heather clawed out from under snow;

mittens too precious, tore the heather loose
in that weather. The bare malformed hands,
nails curved, grew flesh like smoked wood.

Under an open sky, such fuel burned too fast;
in the snow-house, the walls would soften —
worse, smoke trouble the house's master.

She lay, low, to cook in a flat hut with a hole
in its roof. Blow! Blow! The ashes flew
into her mane, her red mongoose eyes.

To eat is good. To trap, to kill, to drive
the dogs' ferocity is heroic to tell:
full-bellied sagas' stuff.

The clawing for heather, the black curved nails,
cramped breath for smoke, smoke for breath,
the witch mask clamped on the bride face

bring nothing, but life for the nourished.
Poor cannibals; we eat what we can:
it is honorable to sustain life.

By her breath, flesh, her hands, no
reputation will be made, no
saga descend. It is only the

next day made possible.

The Fittest

When the great dust
has settled, settled completely
and the air
completely is soundless,
he will be there.
In his neat thousands
will move.

Poor cockroach
he will be blind,
not sterile. His seed, his galaxy
of seed
will shine and rustle,
blind but agile.

Where a child's elbow
curved, where a man
spoke and moved
where bird and woman sang
will come his shining rustle:
where the rose
sprang from its green stem.

The Night Watchman

A small light, furtive, peers,
picks out a palm bole,
breadfruit green as a snake.
The night watchman is on his rounds, his right arm
heavy with its thousand years.

The dark keeps space behind
his left shoulder. For a moment
on my white wall in a white square
shadows of palm fronds struggle
with the invisible wind.

The Caribbean has taken back
its colors: the broken moon
scatters its steps on black. Here cocks
crow all night and dogs that slept
in the sedative sun, bark, bark, bark.

I ask of the watchman the seasoned
question: What of the night? From what
will he protect me? Other questions:
Where did she go? Is the mongoose
nocturnal? What should we have done?

Dogged as cock or dog, his light will return.
Protection! Protection? While
the thin knives of the clock
shred minute by minute, and the sea
turns over its bones?

It Is the Season

   when we learn
or do not learn
to say goodbye . .

The crone leaves that, as green
virgins, opened themselves
to sun, creak at our feet

and all farewells return
to crowd the air:
say, Chinese lovers by a bridge,

with crows and a waterfall;
he will cross
the bridge, the crows fly;

children who told each other
secrets, and will not speak
next summer.

Some speech of parting
mentions God, as in
Adieu, Adios,

commending what cannot
be kept
to permanence.

There is nothing of north
unknown, as the dark
comes earlier. The birds

take their lives in their wings
for the cruel trip.
All farewells are rehearsals.

Darling, the sun rose
later today.
Summer, summer

is what we had.
Say nothing yet.
Prepare.

Figure

for William Meredith

Out of the bone landscape
of stone and sand, a man
on a burro appears

alone, distant;
egg for head, stick arms,
stick legs, out of all years

of the sand, the stone; going
to no seen spot, confers
a human form on the eye

before he vanishes
as though bony distance
had eaten him.

Nothing is like him. Vulnerable,
he has not profited
from the feral faunal data:

the yellow crab spider
on golden rod; the brown
beetle on soil; the katy-

did on its green leaf;
the delectable Viceroy
mimicking the acrid Monarch. Outwit,

or lie low and wait. The cock-
roach, in 300 million
years has not seen fit

to change. Yet durability
cannot be said
to be all. Nor fear.

The stony bony sandy view
shifted itself, focused
upon him till he left it there.